A Doctor Pedalled Her Bicycle
Over the River Arno

A Doctor Pedalled Her Bicycle Over the River Arno

Matt Rader

poems

ANANSI

This edition published in 2011 by
House of Anansi Press Inc.
110 Spadina Avenue, Suite 801
Toronto, ON, M5V 2K4
Tel. 416-363-4343
Fax 416-363-1017
www.anansi.ca

Distributed in Canada by
HarperCollins Canada Ltd.
1995 Markham Road
Scarborough, ON, M1B 5M8
Toll free tel. 1-800-387-0117

Distributed in the United States by
Publishers Group West
1700 Fourth Street
Berkeley, CA 94710
Toll free tel. 1-800-788-3123

House of Anansi Press is committed to protecting our natural environment.
As part of our efforts, this book is printed on paper that contains 100%
post-consumer recycled fibres, is acid-free, and is processed chlorine-free.

15 14 13 12 11   1 2 3 4 5

LIBRARY AND ARCHIVES CANADA CATALOGUING IN PUBLICATION

Rader, Matt, 1978–
A doctor pedalled her bicycle over the River Arno / Matthew Rader.

Poems.
ISBN 978-0-88784-255-9

I. Title.

PS8585.A2825D63 2011   C811'.6   C2010-906475-5

Library of Congress Control Number: 2010940721

Cover design: Bill Douglas
Typesetting: Sari Naworynski

We acknowledge for their financial support of our publishing program
the Canada Council for the Arts, the Ontario Arts Council,
and the Government of Canada through the Canada Book Fund.

Printed and bound in Canada

The night we crossed the border
The freeway, where it met sky,
Disappeared into a bruise of light.

From the oncoming headlights
I snaffled for you a string of pearls
To put around your pearly neck.

Contents

Music

I awoke on Veteran's Day in the United States
To blue skies and a republican Cali sunshine
That made the whole town of McKinleyville
Appear lit from the inside, as if it were its own
Source of light, as if it still heard the sad music
Of its first name, Minor, and heard the minor
Third McKinley sang when he was shot through
The stomach and the pancreas and the kidney
At the Temple of Music in Buffalo, New York
In nineteen hundred and one. We were talking
Poetry, my friend and me, and what happened
To the lake in Blue Lake after the Mad River
Was leveed and how McKinley was the last
Veteran of the Civil War elected President,
How he died of gangrene because the surgeons
Had been forced to operate by reflected sun-
Light and could not find the bullet. We talked
As we drove the back roads of Humbolt County
About our faith in the persistent wellspring
Of meaning and sang along with Springsteen,
Headed north to the tall trees at Prairie Creek,
Past the beachhead at Trinidad and the casino
And the Orick gas bar, past the present moment
Into our late afternoon beer at the Fieldbrook
General Store where we sat in the dimness
And recalled things that happened long before
Us like the redwood forest and the salt marsh
In Humbolt Bay, like the Pan-American Expo
Where the first x-ray machine was on display
And President McKinley reached out to shake
The hand of a man carrying a pistol concealed
By a handkerchief. "All my people are larger
Bodies than mine," my friend quoted Agee,

3

"By some chance, here they are, all on this earth."
These are the facts as I know them. McKinley
Died from a lack of light and the assassin
Was executed by electricity on State Street
In Auburn, New York, on the traditional land
Of the Iroquois Confederacy, two weeks before
A wrecking crew razed the Temple of Music.

"All my people are larger bodies than mine, quiet, with voices gentle and meaningless like the voices of sleeping birds . . . By some chance, here they are, all on this earth . . . Remember them kindly in their time of trouble; and in the hour of their taking away."

James Agee, *A Death in the Family*

The Latin for Hunger

The year they uncovered our three-year-old
Neighbour silent in the wooded easement
Behind her apartment, I learned to identify
Those trees by the Latin, *alnus rubra*,
Red alder, the first taker of disturbed lands.
That year, my brother, who was only nine,
Stopped eating and I fell madly in love
With a Jewish girl whose skin was so white
It was almost not there and whose blue eyes
Were so blue the red in them remembered
The flight from Egypt, the moonscape
Of Sinai, the artist with his broken hand
Drawing in the dark at Terezin, and more
I never had the heart to decipher. That year
A large boy held the three-year-old girl
In his arms while I read "A Hunger Artist"
And learned how denial could be a form
Of luxury, the slow emergence of the artist's
Ribs slipping the bars of his cell. My brother
Grew thinner and thinner all through Lent
And into Passover when I attended my first
Seder at the home of the fair Jewish girl
I'd met, finally, in twelfth grade biology.
The food was almost edible, almost normal.
For some reason, all through dinner and after
I kept thinking about the red inner flesh
Of the alder and my brother and that girl,
The one in the woods with our neighbour,

The neighbour girl whose crooked neck
Seemed to point to something outside
Of herself, which was outside my brother
Too, but not me. I'd already taken in
Too much of the world. According to Kafka
When the public will no longer attend
The spectacle of the artist's hunger, his art
Is dead. *Alnus rubra*, then *acer rubrum*,
Then red cedar, whose Latin name I can not
For the life of me remember: the sequence
Of succession in the Northwest forests.
That year I saw a Jewish girl, undressed,
Lay the white lamb of herself upon her bed
And my youngest brother in the white shroud
Of hospital linens under a copse of poles
And plastic bladders. The neighbour boy,
Unattended in his cell, escaped himself
One night, later that year, while the guards
Watched television. I pressed my lean body
Into the lean body of that girl and entered
History at a point that turned all mine in
Front of me. Trussed with tubes and fluids
My brother got stronger against his will
And in the late summer when the air held
A deep blue that grew darker every day
He came home, thin, almost himself again.

Gravity & Grace

The air unravels at Cape Canaveral
and in Oregon a rain-rattle in the gutter
like chariots on cobblestone — Cape
Kennedy, you insist, canaveral being
a canebrake, a snake able to paralyze
the lungs with its spit of neurotoxin,
a vast tract overtaken by sugarcane.

The Second Born

A quiet ordeal. No gob of gawkers on the second go.
Only the slobber-faced firstborn
With the goat horn rattle and the goat
With one horn, the carpenter and the gobsmacked girl on her back
In the barn goading the little god out of her
Through the open gate of her hips into the open ark

Of straw and shit and manger mud, the pre-electric dark
No single star in night's vast archipelago
Of stars saw fit to mark as strange or special or simply other
As it had, once before, for the brother, that stubborn
Gob of flesh now akimbo the back
Of Joe, the Carpenter. A family affair. The one-horned goat

Going down on his knees — a sacrificial goat
If we please — so Joe can trace with his callused thumb the arch
Of the horn all the way back
To that first night on the lam with a pregnant wife, so long ago
Now it's like another life forborne
By another bloke, a better one, a better father,

Step-father, earth-father,
Whatever title the Lord's scapegoat
Deserves for being there when the child was born
If, alas, not much before. The mark
Of a good man. The logo
And logos of a fellow who works with his hands — Cut back

And the girl's gilded with sweat and grime and on her back,
Gonzo, ready to give up, give in, give her
The old heave-ho and go
AWOL in her mind all the way back to before the goat
Lost its first horn, before the first spark
Of pain in her womb was born,

Before the first pomegranate seed borne
On the tongue of Persephone promised her and half the year to
    Hades, back
To a first mythology where the Ark
Of Heaven was housed in the sepulchre of her
Body and boy, the carpenter and the goat
With one horn who does not flinch when his last is the first to go

In celebration of the newborn, a birthmark
Any beast would bear and go forth gladly, uncrowned, a goat
With no horns at the back of the barn, bare before her.

from **Reservations**

1. K'ÓMOKS, VANCOUVER ISLAND

We'd miss it if we could, that quarter-hour
Drive to the next town west for groceries
Or theatre, a restaurant dinner, *la carte du jour*
Of needs and entertainments we'd disease
Ourselves with until compelled to travel.
When we did make the trip we made it quick,
Cursing the slow native cruise of traffic
We navigated in search of the new and novel
Beyond our village. Whatever reservations
We harboured we harboured in our cars
As we toured seaside and Reservation,
And chose to keep our thoughts ours
On local decor, jalopies, the giant whale maw
Big House door. Out of respect, of course. And awe.

Freaks, Irregulars, Defects, Oddities

An ill-minted coin, a monocle
    Chained to a tuxedo,
The moon croons to strip-clubs,
    And late-night burrito

Shops, lovers on pedicab tours
    Of the harbour. Placido
Domingo on the stereo with merlot
    And fettuccine alfredo.

A night for werewolves, hairy
    Men sporting speedos
And high heels on the club stroll,
    "The Streets of Laredo"

On ukulele and pennywhistle
    Down at the lido
Where a shot-wrecked Aeneas
    Meets his new Dido.

Virgil, installed in a corner stall
    Puts pen to graffito:
"Tally-ho! Damn the torpedoes!
    Bandita hearts Bandito!"[1]

Oh, tragic pyred Queen of Tyre,
    It's Fido not Dido
That translates as faithful,[2]
    The "Fido"-fido credo

On love Dante witnesses mid-canto
    When Aeneas snubs Dido
In the second circle where she's been unjustly gaoled
    For her raging — [3]

Now Freaks, Irregulars, Defects, Oddities,
    People of the low, low albedo,
Let this be your motto:
    "Love" the word not the weirdo.

---

[1]Virgil's friend Dante's best Fido
    Was "A Lady Loves Me" author Calvacanti, Guido.
[2]"Testicle," to the Roman tongue, sounded out "orchido."
    [3]Spanish Guy Fawkes goes by Fawkes, Guido.

Indulgence

With you on your knees between my knees
I see The Cruelty of Achilles when Priam came
To recover Hector's body and the old king,
Like you, used his lips to please his enemy,

Or that last scene from von Stroheim's *Greed*
In the heart of Death Valley, where McTeague,
Alone with the gold, goes down on his knees
On the caked ground and cracked alkaline

Next to his dead mule and empty canteen,
Cuffed to the corpse of his former ally, free
At last to be pitied and die in the desert heat.
How could we with shame and devotion?

The penitent pilgrim kneeling the Holy Steps
Skims years of indulgences with each ascent.
I rise to you, an unspoken syllable that fills
Your mouth, makes everything unspeakable.

from **Reservations**

2. 'KSAN HISTORICAL VILLAGE, HAZELTON

"How you fixed for rooms?" he'd begin
As if about to launch a pitch for a set,
Then add, "two beds, no smoking, no pets,"
An order my father would score no bargain
On this long weekend. "Good," they said,
Or "Bad," depending on how they heard
The question. It meant the same: no beds
Where we were asking and let words be words.
So there we stood in the village parking lot,
On the confluence of two northern rivers,
With no reservations, facing the thought
Of a night in the truck. To be reserved,
I confirmed, taciturn. Native or nonnative,
It's the only way to thole and live, let live.

Empire Days

The spring I returned
To my village
On the Salish Sea,

Each blue afternoon
The moon followed me
Home from work.

When I walked
Down Main Street
In the soft rain

Only strangers
In their warm Japanese
Vehicles stopped

To ask directions
And who was I
To withhold the way!

I was shown kindness
By the barber
Who spoke less and less

As he cut the hair from my head
And it fell
Like a hush over the tiles.

To be as feted as I was
And widely loved
By mosquitoes and rust!

Even clouds celebrated
With lightning
And thunder. Feast days

On the main drag,
I held my daughter's hand
In horror

Before fire engines,
Classic cars,
Veterans of Hitler's War.

Body of Work
i.m. Otto Van Barneveld

When on the cardboard factory fell Allied bombs
It was not like Brueghel's Icarus for the Dutch
Prisoner who would become my grandfather,
For nobody went on assembling boxes in silence
And what falling through the roof that prisoner saw
Was not a boy but a whole sky of black wombs
In search of their boys. Not to the Old Masters
Did his boyish mind turn but to the church
Tower of Barneveld and Cpt. Jan van Schaffelaar
Who with great composure from the tower leapt
To save his men the trouble. Jan van Schaffelaar,
Do not weep for that Dutch prisoner from whom
I plucked your name. For when you ceased falling
He walked free into the German night and kept
Walking, the ploughman from Brueghel's painting
For whom, the Old Master tells us, the failure was not
Failure enough to stop the sunshine or the ploughing.

Natural Lives
For Nora, b. April 7, 2009

Headed headlong toward the white light
Of the midwife's palms you arrived lacquered
In nacre, iridescent, almost see-through

For a second, as if the mother-of-pearl
Blue that blushed back as soon as you
Unstoppered your first breath, first hue

And cry for your own unmediated oxygen,
Recalled the milky wash of stars and carbon,
Our elemental origins. I was thirty-one

For the first time the day you were born
On the white-tile bathroom floor and placed
By the midwife on first your mother's bare

White chest then mine. And we'll go on,
You and I, marking each age for the first time
On that same calendar day in early April

When an ambulance arrived with a wail
At my grandfather's door, white body awash
In washed reds and blues, to bear him

From his home for the last time. We'll share
That day, you and I, all our natural lives.

from **Reservations**

3. 19 WING, CFB COMOX

A carpet of tarmac, grass. A welcome mat
For swans in winter, seagulls, crows, aircraft,
Whatever creature could not motor and draft
Enough reserve commitment to combat
Gravity, wind, the economics of force
V. force along the northwest coast.
Tacked to the peninsula by metal posts,
Chain-link, a barbed-wire telephone cord
That delivered a code we heard into words —
"Keep out," it said, "keep back, keep to yourself" —
The place became a preserve for wild birds
Who set down and settled on the runway, safe
Behind the lines of their closest human cousins,
To reserve and re-serve under better conditions.

Ocean's Love to Oregon

Laying open craggy Oregon, Quadra
Backs a Tillamook girl to a rock
As the Pacific backs beach to cliff-face

Then surges against her into the mouth
Columbia, plashing her long neck, her caves
And coves caressed into shape

By his tongue, till all his ringlets are
Breathless sweat and scent blessing her linens
Of sand like incense, mist, lifting

*

Her cedar-bark skirt to her breasts,
Quadra drives north into unknown channels,
Seeding his *lengua* on stony outcrops

To germinate in the *oscuro* sea
Of bleeding Madrone, *Punta de los Martires*,
Islas de Ladrones, Boca de Bodega,

Where the dugout of the Tillamook
Heaves upon each swell, black *culebra* of kelp
Enwombed in the wave-crest, hard

*

Against her, the ocean lays
His head on the ribbed hull of the continent
As Quadra charts the Tillamook

Heartbeat in her chest-nook, the bridge-gap
Of collarbone worn by his listening
In amazement at the synchronicity of the moon-

Pull and his own impulse to retreat
And reclaim the beachhead where he first heard
Her whisper his name: *agua, agua, agua* . . .

Leave the Light On

Because the light in the room where you awaited me
Could be seen from the street and I had come over
Island mountains right when the blue light of afternoon
Made of the sky a blue window into a heavenly room
Where I could see you reading this note five days
In the future, I did not knock before I opened your door.

The Tribes of Snow & Stars

For Moshe & Tamar

Talking with you this early winter evening,
I follow dark Israeli eyes out of the desert
And into the woolly Oregon sky where fall
Millions on millions of one-of-a-kind stars:

The star of David, the star of Bethlehem,
The stars and stripes, and one red star I catch
And gift to you: the leaf of an autumn maple.

Should we to our nativities one day return
May snow be the gold, frankincense and myrrh
I journey with to the Christmas of your minds

As in the window of sky at home I light eight
White snowflakes that burn eight long days,

Until in revolt God tosses his heavenly temple
And once again to earth float the myriad stars.

from **Reservations**

4. KWANTLEN POLYTECHNIC UNIVERSITY

From "Arboreal Burials and Business," in *The Elf*
Of History, or How to Get a Berth
In Course Reserve — that twilight sleep,
As doctors say, of pedagogical urgency —
"Bodies boxed up and shelved on the top shelf
Of a tree with enough height and girth
To support a family of slaves. To keep,
As priests say, their spiritual currency."
It comes to mind en route to class this fall
As wind bends the campus trees like bows
And hurtles branches across the quadrangle:
A femur, a clavicle, an ossuary of arrows
Turned sticks pointing past the concrete
To dirt and beasts, the complete and incomplete.

Train to Brisbane

On pause and alone in the languid pulse
    Of a passenger car, my eye-cogs
Re-pattern the gum groves and poulticed
    Pastures, the grey grainy smog

Of darkness and heat dawn-light dusts
    From the green mantle of Earth's
Southern room, into a distant Italian dusk
    Accruing like soot upon the hearth

Of a day before this latest war, our train
    Trembling like Attila's horses
Through Roman suburbs, the airplanes
    Departing Da Vinci on course

For London, Prague, Stuttgart, crucifixes
    Hoisted on night's worn shoulder —
Tell me, are you afflicted too, cursed by fits
    Of cross-traffic when one order

Suddenly overtakes another? — A tremor
    In the picture, a jab and judder
As the entire train whelms and now-or-
    Never lurches into near future

Where a scrim of smokestacks wheels on
    To the backstage of horizon,
And I am gathered again on a slow train
    In the lowlands west of Brisbane.

Worldchanging

The spoor of the civet cat
You flushed from its foxhole
Behind the fridge stayed
For weeks, growing
Less and less vivid each day
Until it disappeared completely
Into us and our ordinary.

Party Politics

One hundred horses out to graze and gallivant
In bad weather got landlocked in the North Atlantic —

The Lough Atlantic on a recent Dutch schematic
Sent to Irish Parliament (now that Irish Parliament
Is Irish again), laying out plans for further development

The two governments might go Dutch on (a pint
Of Guinness and a tongue sandwich — I'll give you a hint:
What is lunch for the Dutch-Irish?) but won't or can't

Until the horses are back. The damn rabble don't give a damn
About dikes or dams or steel super-structures to hold back
The sea around Venice, Italy. It's horses, horses, horses.

And of course it is. Send in the army. Parry and attack.
The Atlantic can't hold out forever, good sir. Sorry, Madam.
Need spurs? Rope? Carrot on a stick? Cart for the horses?

*

Need spurs? Rope? Carrot on a stick? Cart for the horses?
Ms. Atlantica can't hold out forever, good sir. Sorry, Madam.
And of course it is. Serve in the army. Marry and attack.

You see, around Venice Beach it's all horses, horses, horses!
About dykes and dams and rubber super-structures . . . hold back.
Until the horses are black, the damn rabble won't give a damn.

What's for lunch? Four butch-Irish? I won't. I can't —
Oh, Guinness and a tongue-sandwich it is. Get the hint?
Might we two governments go Dutch on a pint

Of Irish again? "Laying" out plans for further "development"?
A "seat" in Irish parliament? — yes, *that* parliament —
Look, Atlantica, a Dutch oven! Smegmatic!

I'm bad weather locked-in. Got north? Anal attic?
One hundred out horses! Graze, man. Gallivant.

from **Reservations**

5. GUANTÁNAMO BAY, CUBA
For Omar Khadr

A hostel for a host of hostiles, the base
Plays host to a gallery of insurgents and rogues,
Both native and non-native, from across the globe —
Royal Poinciana, for one,
A.k.a., *flamboyan.*
For two, the Canada goose.
But it's the pomegranate, Omar, that makes me think of you,
The so-called "first fruit" — *la grenade,*
As they say *en français* —
Courtesy a dint of watering by an American crew,
The ordnance grows into a dull red globe, a kind of third-world
Christmas bauble, across the yard where I imagine
They're keeping you, and have been ever since you hurled
That pomegranate in Ayub Kheyl, Afghanistan.

Chinatown

Perseverance Creek Heritage Site, Cumberland, BC

I.

Between borehole number four and number three,
In the bubbly fug and fen with cattails, frogspawn,
The skunk cabbage calling back the dried fungi

II.

And sea-things on Keefer Street or North Beach
Or the Bowery, my fondness for films by Polanski,
Down in the deeper cover with coal and prejudice,

III.

I spot Mah Fun among the alder and salmonberry,
Slag-faced, relieved, giddy to get above ground,
Taking a leak behind the Chinese National League,

IV.

A teapot tucked under his arm as if expecting me
To step through the trees, to join him in the swamp
Of history for a good bullshit and bitter cup of tea,

V.

His yellow stream yellowing the earth at his feet
And my feet, the sun and the swamp lantern flower.

I Acknowledge

I acknowledge I am on the unceded traditional land of the
K'ómoks nation.

I do not speak their language.

I acknowledge Wednesday is garbage day in the Comox Valley.

I speak English. *C'est la.*

I acknowledge the Department of National Defence shooting range
on Goose Spit, K'ómoks territory, is over one hundred years old.

This guy owed me money.

I acknowledge the right of K'ómoks band members to access their
traditional burial grounds on Goose Spit with proper identification.

My father spoke Dutch.

My father's father spoke Dutch.

I acknowledge every other Wednesday is recycling.

Sathloot, Sasitla, Ieeksun, Puntledge, Cha'chae, Tat'poos

— the tribes of "the land of plenty,"

a.k.a. the Comox Valley.

I acknowledge my inability to pronounce these names.

I was driving by the Quinsam Hotel when I saw his car in the parking lot.

My mother's father spoke Italian.

I acknowledge the man between my wife's knees is not me. I like it. I so acknowledge.

I was schooled in K'ómoks Territory. I have the words of only this new family.

I dragged that fucker to the curb and opened two cans of Lucky.

I acknowledge my ungrateful ways.

I acknowledge the proposed treaty right of the K'ómoks First Nation to construct a hotel and conference centre on Goose Spit, Comox, British Columbia.

Only trust those who are not afraid to get sloppy.

I acknowledge Gawd Almitee and the Grate Spearit.

I am guilty. I have no guilt. I do not believe in property.

I believe in propriety.

I have everything backwards. I have what I have. I give it away.

Every other Wednesday is yard waste.

A Halloween Mask

When he drew his hood and became the grey
Ancestor fallen out of place in the long march
Of evolution, brooding, mute, without change
Of mood, the mask dissolved to reveal his true face.
Our true face who hold a void near our hearts.
What he was supposed to be she could not say.

Ablution

i.m. S. L.

I.

Because the bathtub was as full of you
As evenings when you washed yourself
And your long blonde hair and brushed
It out before bed, we cleaned carefully,
My young wife and me, on our knees,
As if sponge bathing your absent body.

II.

Before offering a prayer or taking a life
One must be good and of pure condition:
Feet, thighs and inner thighs, the genitals,
Pubic hair, buttocks, belly and breasts,
Right arm, left arm, fingers, fingernails,
Neck, the nostrils, ears, teeth, tongue, hair.

III.

Tonight, when I draw my daughters' bath,
Brush their hair, their tiny teeth, perform
The evening ritual to prepare for sleep,
The running water runs all the way back
To your brimming body and damp hair
As I held your head to wipe underneath.

IV.

Undress: take the chain from the neck,
The gold from the ears, uncuff the fingers
And arrange the rings like an alphabet
On the bedside table, remove the cotton
That covers the skin, let down the hair:
Brushings will begin with a cedar bough.

V.

Out of the thousands of times I have lain
Naked with my wife, her brown hair falling
Across my face, her thighs open to a page
From the Heroides, I confess to one time
In our early lives when I imagined her
Body was your body moving above me.

VI.

There comes a darkness on the Salish Sea
So modest that when we stand without
Clothes on a moonless beach we cannot
See each other's bodies and so revealing
That when we enter we see the water
Climax with the white light of basic life.

VII.

Because she loved you as much as me
My wife pulled your hair from the drain
In the tub, from the tines of your brush
And from the mirror wiped your finger-
Prints so as to help complete your dying
Wish to leave and let us get on with it.

from **Reservations**

6. Yuquot (Friendly Cove), Nootka Sound

Unruled and unrailed, ten feet above
The spot where Maquinna kept
John Jewitt, the blacksmith slave,
At work on rusted rifle stocks
And knife blades, the unfinished church deck stuck out over rocks
And weeds, wobbly and free, like the child
Of Maquinna who toddled
Unreservedly over its open concept.
Or maybe I made up the bit about Jewitt
And the exact placement of the deck —
Years later, I can still see her neck
Whiplash when she hit
But can't picture anything more about the fall.
Only her hopping up, unharmed, starting to bawl.

Present & Future

Present: (Under him rolls the globe.)

Future: Trees and mountains wheel
          Beneath my feet.

P: (Spires and smokestacks reel
    Like staggered prize fighters on the ropes of the horizon
    As the sea staggers under the heel of moon and sun
    Suicides in the sea.)
F: Nose to nose I meet you in the garden
    Of today's irradiated haze, in the sick foliage of Eden
    As you've come to know it and know it not. Take your hands
    From your face and face me.
P: Faceless, I am what stands
    As your wake, what wakes only to this moment
    And knows nothing else. This soil is our covenant
    And it collects everything: tithings of rain and snow,
    Root scripts, the tatters of wedding gowns fruit trees throw
    From their shoulders in spring . . .
F: The bell of no hour claps
    But does not applaud. All towers bemoan collapse,
    Then collapse right off like Mary beneath the Cross
    Or Pheidippides at Athens' feet. Gain is the road to loss.
P: Your hunger consumes you. Let it be. Even in death's repose
    This breath-petalled window between us will not open or close
    But for an instant and instants are mine alone.
F: No glass
    But this wind, the plate of air we're pressed against.
P: Pass
    Then black wind into my lung's slack sails. Carry me away.
F: I have come for you. I am coming. I will come. Any day.

Homeowner's Manual

Through each door we walked through I'd look
For you doing all the things you like to do
When no one has eyes on you —
Thumb *Cosmo*, search YouTube, flip a dirty book
On urban chicken coops, a finger or two
Of ice and gin and tonic, free hand down
Your pants, unbuttoned, relaxed, the dressing gown
Of afternoon dressing and undressing you —
So when I saw you pressed against
The butcher block countertop and sunlight
Sheer over your shoulders, I knew
I'd give all my money to live here with you
And hide my eyes from time to time so you might
Go inside yourself, sense what I have sensed.

Promethean
For Neela

The strawberry in your tiny hands
Is larger than your heart but not
More red or sacred. You will not
Eat it, but instead lift it like a flame

To my lips. Behind the strawberry's
Red eye, your own baby blue eyes
Measure me as Diogenes' lantern
Measures men's hearts. I open the gate

Of my teeth and into my darkness
You feed the flame. I am left raw
With strawberry juice and flesh

As you remove the lantern light
From my mouth and to your own
Lips raise the fruit, my stolen heart.

from **Reservations**

7. The Maid of the Mist, Niagara Falls, Ontario

A veil, a shroud, a pall over it all:
The boat, the cataract, the Sheraton Niagara Falls
Where we will repair
With wet glasses and hair
Once we've seen everything there is to see
In this border country
Between blind rage
And blind
(As if there's any other kind)
Duty to go forward and change
Everything. The hotel, I'm told, changed the airflow
Above the falls and now
Even the best views from boat or building or street
Are wound in a winding sheet.

Clearcut

For Brian Young

It's times like these, comrade, in the clearcut
of a quiet bar, beer untroubled on the table,
the waitress, who, a moment earlier, flit over
my shoulder, flit off now for a smoke or pee,
the barkeep taking the opportunity to stand
in the doorway and survey the main drag
for this afternoon's particular brand of solitude,

that I think of us legging it out of the trees,
half-slouched, the only beasts beastly enough
to interrupt the stillness of the clearcut,
the instinct of the lower species to hesitate
at open space and case the edge for enemies
distinctly absent in us as we cut into the cut
and crossed among the stumps and blackberry.

Would you believe I heard two voices that day
above the valley? One said, "Mean and be
mean. Name everything. The world is yours
to itemize and recite, cleave and cleave to
with language." The other said, "To sanction
or be sanctioned. Be particular but be multiple.
Draw the line that defines you and step over."

It was just then we paused to catch our breath
on the spine of the ridge. I turned to look
at who had joined us on the rise, had fallen in
step on our slow ascent up the mangled hillside.
Across the strait a blue-black slate of geology
smoked like cardice. You know as well as I.
One voice was yours, comrade. One mine.

— Cumberland, BC

Loosestrife

Loose in loosestrife and knotweed,
the suck and thunk
of bootsteps in nitrogen drunk,
ocean sluiced, tidal mud —
We come together with cutters
to cull roots, to sink
our hands in weedy muck
and shuck purple heralds
from the arms of the earth,
snaffle foreign flags
flown here in the guts of waterfowl
or snarled like garland
and piggybacked on boat props
to propagate and invade outland veins,
brackish ditches, fenland,
the gabbled brook that feeds the fallow field
swans forage in for grubs,
or to choke the open estuary mouth.
We pluck bouquets of the crinkly weed
from the briny wash
to dangle like catkins
in the kitchen window, a warder
against gnats and mosquitoes,
or placed in the basket between us,
as on the yoke of quarrelsome beasts,
a wild purple warrant for peace.

Weeds

For A. M.

A disturbed script of scrawny tangle, unkempt
Next to our raised beds, those carefully staked
And allotted garden plots we tend and attend to
Like parents of perfected children. Unrequited,
It makes advances over borders we outlined
With bamboo posts and garden twine, libidinous,
Stubborn, recalcitrant, as if it too has a mind
To make things right and after its own image.

On hands and knees in the open earth summer
Evenings when weeds are touched and dug up:
We know what we know by what we reject.
So let speak all things that go without saying
Like weeds return new to the vegetable garden.
May no words be the last word on any subject.

from **Reservations**

8. TSAWWASSEN FERRY TERMINAL, DELTA

For fifteen bucks and change (nearly a pack
Of smokes these days), I saved myself
A spot on the crossing. Reserved,
We might say, as the ferry corp. does, a berth
On-board the boat that will take me back
Home. *The Spirit of*
Vancouver Island, they call her
(A "spirit class" vessel,
Where "class" means kind and "spirit" girth). At the terminal,
We cue up in our cars, get out, get coffee, relieve ourselves,
Await the voice we've heard how many times before tell
Us to return to our vehicles
In preparation for boarding. I am ready to go.
I get the signal. I go.

Customs

For Karen Ford,

In the last days of our republics
Our customs long forgotten
And weeds and wildflowers
Come for our land, my people
Will ford the old border river
And name the pithy berries
On the opposite bank, karen.

"Sto:lo culprit in the murder of 'Captain' Bell of Whatcom . . .
Very short work will be made of [Louis Sam] . . ."

The British Columbian, Wednesday, February 27th, 1884

"Caught on the British side of the line . . . Hence
Entrusted to Thomas York of Sumas . . . to be tried for the offence . . .

Folly to put the county to unnecessary expense . . .
A little Seattle justice . . . a salutary effect . . . common sense . . ."

Whatcom Reveille, Wednesday, February 27th, 1884

"Latest:
A crowd of good citizens took [Sam]
From guards on the York homestead and hung him.
No cost."

Whatcom Reveille, Thursday, February 28th, 1884

"From a family of bad Indians . . . To wit
Few regrets wasted upon the suddenness of [Sam's] exit."

The British Columbian, Saturday, March 1st, 1884

After dawn they cut him down
    From that border tree.
Thomas York took hold the feet
    And when the corpse came free
He let it fall into his arms,
    A faggot of kindling,
Light and straight and bony thin,
    A boy become a thing.

With open eyes the thing did see
    The skin upon the face
That rolled it in a tablecloth
    And cinched the dark in place.
With death-filled ears the thing did hear
    A man begin to sing,
As he lifted it upon a horse,
    "A boy become a thing."

And did they set it in the ground
    Or bury it in fire
Or did they leave it on a rock
    To build a buzzard pyre?
The record here goes deaf and dumb.
    The song refuses to sing.
Louis Sam's his English name.
    A boy become a thing.

A Voice from the Posse, Vancouver, 19xx

We'd hardly put Bell to bed when we lit out,
The sexton still folding earth over the Captain,
Tucking him in to await his reckoning. About
Dusk we met up, near every able-bodied man
In Whatcom on horseback and gussied right
In skirts and eye make-up outside Osterman's.
The papers said we rode north by moonlight
But it wasn't so. Was a dark night for certain.
A night of no moon. Moultray, the politician,
Painted a red slash over his eyes that flashed
In the torchlight, his little mouth set in a grin.
"A posse of good citizens has gone washed
This county clean of one more renegade Indian."
And "I'd kill a Chinaman as plain as I'd kill
An Indian and I'd kill an Indian just as plain
As I'd kill a dog." That kind of talk up trail
But a good piece of silence too. In His eyes
We'd have looked not unlike fire ants at work
On the black carcass of the Earth, a surmise
Of small men in procession through murk
And witchgrass, the wet musk cedars censer
Our winters with clinging to us as we left
The trail and crossed, one by one, the border.
Of thoughts in life I've too often been bereft,
And I'd not thought the boy would recognize
Us, our faces hooded in dark and kerchiefs,
But when Harkness noosed him his injin eyes
Flared wide as dollars and before we thiefed
His life he spoke, clear and calm: "I see you
Bill Moultray. I see you and I'm going to

Get you and you and you." I been looked through
Before but that boy saw the very inner doings
Of me and still more. Like he saw Moultray
Clear as day in the dark, he saw each one of us
Who'd come to hang him up. We betrayed
The Devil himself in that deed and we trussed
Him in that cedar to show his redskinned kin
What white men will do to protect the Good.
Few years after we were annexed to the Union,
And Bill got Senator for this neck of the woods.

Thomas York to L. Sam, Sumas Lake, 188x

From drink, at dayligone,
I hear iron-shod horses
Rattle the earth outside.
Shakes me. The night divorces.
I hurt, I go, I hide
In hundred proof what's done.

Here daughter. And here wife.
My son asleep between.
Oil-light unmasks my face
A moment, hard and lean.
I drink in drink's embrace
But how it cleaves my life.

And you in from the wood.
You sit at my table
Noosed in the night's dark blues
And flicker, unstable.
I pour a glass, toast you.
My gut growl-gripes for food.

Last night, I wrung a goose,
Bled it behind the shed.
I smell my hands, heat-soak'd,
My wife's warm, crowded bed,
And you — rope, ghost of smoke,
Gun metal, cedar. Truce.

You come here to frustrate
My work, my sleep, my drink.
I take my whiskey hard.
You stare and do not blink.
The horses stamp the yard.
This food cold on my plate.

MRS. FRASER YORK SPEAKS TO MAJOR MATTHEWS,
SUMAS LAKE, 1945

You could hardly see it from the road,
Our little house, beneath a bower of roses

And the white parasols of acacia trees
Father York planted in the eighties,

From saplings — come from Africa those
Trees, you know that? No one knows

Or cares to remember but we all come
From somewhere and mostly that some-

Where wasn't here. Except them cedars.
They've been encamped on this land years.

They have generations of weather and earth
Etched into their boles. Except the hearth

And the chimney, which are river stone,
The whole house is cedar. Everyone

Who's been inside feels it a heady odour.
Everything, the walls, the joists, the door,

All of it yellow cedar. Yes, we are free
Of bugs in this redolence. Believe me,

Everything about Fraser smelled of cedar
When I met him: his skin, his black hair,

His parents, Thomas and Anna Maria,
Who he resembled, it's true, like a mirror.

It becomes part of you. It goes deep. I got
Used to it quick enough and then forgot

About it much of the time. That's how
It was then: get used to it, fast or slow,

But get used to it and go on like a clock,
Steady. Continuous. No need to talk.

As the Sto:lo Gather for War, the Fraser River Speaks, 1884

My course is set. I go in one direction only:
To the sea. I ruin the earth in my image.
Sons and daughters, do you see me?
My course is set. I go in one direction only
And to whosoever fears not catastrophe
My body can make fleet from here your passage.
My course is set. I go in one direction only:
To the sea. I ruin the earth in my image.

Do you see me, sons and daughters?
See, whosoever fears not catastrophe
I will bear upon the litter of my broken waters.
Do you see me, sons and daughters,
Who will ferry you to ruin and slaughter
Should you set your course mistakenly?
You will see me, sons and daughters,
And tell whosoever fears not catastrophe.

From ruin into ruin this river will ferry you
And make fleet passage from your body
To a vast body of blue and blue and blue.
From ruin into ruin this river will ferry you
Swiftly, my sons and daughters. Retreat to
The trees. Escape the shadow of catastrophe.
Or from ruin into ruin this river will ferry you
And make fleet passage from your body.

The boy each evening climbs into the tree
    And hangs himself, a ridge rope
        Around the neck
    Of the night. Each day I check
The well for water. Each day I husband rope
        To horses. I breathe.

When Christ ascended heaven a wind whistled
    Through the cavities in his hands
        And the cedar
    Crucifix trembled. Dear Father,
The workhorse will not obey our commands.
        Our souls are gristled.

I crank the windlass, unspool rope down the well.
    All that winter's cold is huddled
        In the heartwood
    Of those cedars. What I would
Give to him who could, at last, unraddle
        That body from Hell.

RE: CONVERSATION WITH MRS. F. YORK, 1945,
MAJOR MATTHEWS, VANCOUVER CITY ARCHIVIST

Amendments to record: 1. Acacia trees are native
To all continents save Antarctica. 2. The house
We spoke in was not on the site of the murder.
3. That house stood cheek by jowl with the border
And was razed to build the customs office.
4. Fraser York was the first white baby to survive
Birth in this province. 5. "Me-sah-chie Sam"
Was not Louis, but his father, "the bad Indian,"
Who was already serving a term for murder
At the time of his son's troubles. 6. The border
Posed no obstacle to the posse or Sam's kin.
7. Mrs. York served "saddle," not "rack," of lamb.

Who could fail to feel,
Who's lifted this cold and slender figure eight
In his own hands, the pinch and heft of real
    Agony, the bite and weight

    Upon your wrists? The lock
And key have frozen shut over the century
Into a grim grey steel infinity as if to mock
    Our desire for memory

    To be absolved of you.
Only women and boys could wear bracelets
This size. I ask, who could ratify the true
    And untrue in our regrets

    Except ourselves? No less
A man than the hundred who saw you raised
To your death, I come to bear witness,
    See for myself, appraise.

THE ROPE MAKES ITS CASE, SUMAS LAKE, 1884

Good men, let me take the child's head,
   Take the child's head in my coiled arm,
My one coiled arm I make into a bed,
   A coiled bed to sleep him out of harm.
Out of harm, good men, back to earth,
   Back to earth, always, even in his sleep,
In sleep retreat to the hour of his birth,
   His birth into gravity, heavy and deep.
Heavy and deep and a world of harm,
   A world of harm with no wedding bed,
No wedding but the band of my arm,
   My arm, good men, to take his head.

For how long do you expect to stay?
    Any tobacco or firearms to declare?
For how long have you been away?

Date of birth? 1869, Christmas Day?
    Black eyes. Brown skin. Black hair.
For how long do you expect to stay

Employed? Do you swear to obey,
    Worship, say daily the Lord's prayer?
For how long have you been away

From home? Do you suffer decay
    Of flesh or bones? Where do you repair?
For how long do you expect to stay

In that tree? Born of woman or clay?
    Did you claim corpse or cadaver?
For how long have you been away

From your country? Peoples? Body?
    Who will you visit today and where?
For how long do you expect to stay?
    For how long have you been away?

History

I.

That August all along the Yellowhead Highway
As the shadow of our car rippled across
The roadside, and my father and I, at thirty,
Went looking for his past on the Skeena River,
All the tinctures of the north — copper, gold,
Moly blue — bubbled into a carnage of colours
Not even Caravaggio or his Flemish disciple
Could have captured completely: the white
Petals of oxeyes seeping from under the crust
Of the earth like the pustules of lead carbonate
Horrified London curators have uncovered
Pocking the flank of an old master's horse
In the National Gallery; that purple shroud
Of pine trees on the mountainside the beetles
Feasted on and abandoned as those thieves
Of Judea whom the fifth procurator sentenced
To die were abandoned on crude desert trees.
My father loved to drive and he loved wild-
Flowers and when we came upon a hillside
Of complete destruction, obliterated by petals,
He'd stop the conversation but not the car
And we'd float by like time and river water,
Like the Allied shadows that rippled across
The German hayfield where my grandfather
Toiled in the last days of the war by mercy
And pen of an unknown Nazi administrator,
Where everyone, the farmer and prisoners,
Had gone hungry long enough to resemble
One another unmistakably, bare winter trees.
That summer all along the Highway of Tears,
As it's known for the women who have gone

Missing from its shoulders, who have been
Surrendered to absence and in that absence
Become a presence felt by all travellers and me,
Among the paintbrush, buttercup, red clover,
Flared fireweed, also known as evening primrose,
A fine tea. In bomb-pocked London, near the end
Of the war, as my grandfather abandoned the field
He'd been tilling and began his long walk out
Of Germany into northern British Columbia,
There appeared, for the first time in generations,
Fireweed. The same fiery flower that burned
That summer in the ditches all along the highway
As my father and I burned by in search of his
Story which was mine too or so I told myself
As he told me about the fireweed and that other
Summer of his early life, nineteen-fifty-five,
When the Russian landlord took Aunt Allie's door
In lieu of eviction, and that still other summer
When two boys who lived close to my father
Met at a front door a block from his own,
And one carried a rifle and with his finger
Tucked a wildflower in the heart of the other.
The wound of the first home will never close.
Its valleys and terraces darken, its mills spin
Into silence but always a susurrus of wildflowers
Shoals inside us when we are quiet or when
The world is too loud. Hear it in the white
Pox of chemistry in a Rubens or Caravaggio,
In the cinquefoil, figwort and Canada thistle
That simmer in northern ditches and gravel,
Effervesce in the footprints of young women.
On the banks of the Skeena, in a field of grass
And wildflowers where the summer heat lay

Close to the earth and the cold river went on
Without stopping, as it always had, oblivious
To cars and conversation, I abandoned my father
To his childhood, to the middle of the last
Century among daisies and pearly everlasting,
As if he'd never left it, as if the river were
More than historical, as if it could be stopped.

II.

Once, in Firenze, on the Feast of Ferragosto,
When the Assumption of the Blessed Virgin,
The real physical elevation of her sinless soul
And incorrupt body to the Body of Heaven
And the wounded side of her son, is observed
By Holy Obligation, I awoke next to the woman
Who had nursed me as a child and nursed me
Again through that fever-thick August night
In the Old Country where every dark-eyed man
Who made the sign of the cross, the father,
The son, and the holy ghost, at the threshold
Of the Duomo was her own father as he crept
Out of the burning-cold north Pacific Ocean
Into nineteen-forty-four, at the head of a swarm,
One hundred Canadian soldiers disgorged
From the ocean onto the abandoned Aleutian
Shore, frozen and hunched and petrified, sea-
Things, belly down, slithering out of the sea.
All over Italy, Italians were leaving the city
For the beach while I was sick in a third-floor
Pensione, half-delirious for the bottle blonde
At reception who spoke English in a Bronx

Accent as if she'd learned the language from
Martin Scorsese or Francis Ford Coppola,
As if she'd asked me to stay away from her
Simply by speaking words I could understand,
As if by some long-forgotten myth or custom
We were doomed to awaken one night on
Either side of a severed horse head. Tell me,
How could I not want her? How could I not
Cover the shoal of welts across my body
With a white cotton sheet? Beyond the brick
Walls, across the old city, a doctor pedalled
Her bicycle over the River Arno towards me,
Past the Uffizi and the tortured gorgon head
Of Caravaggio, past Museo dell'Opera
Where the hooded face of Nicodemus is
Disguised behind Michelangelo's own visage
Frozen by art in a moment of imagined history
When two men and an unfinished woman
Removed the body of Christ from the cross.
I was sick and I sank deeper into the hollow
In the rented bed. Even Christ, my mother
Said, lay for three days in the tomb of another
Man but she grew so young with every word
That when she finished I was no longer alive,
I had never been born and had never left her,
And everything that was happening to me
Had already happened to someone else who
Was me once before at a later stage of history
But who I would never know. The stranger
In me touched his fingers to my face and felt
The thrum of life beneath the hives. The doctor
Opened her black bag and the whole black
Universe exploded into place: my grandfather

Crawled out of the water and walked on two feet
Into the future, carrying my mother and me
In his shrivelled testicles; Nicodemus returned
Christ to the cross and the cross to the cedar
Of Lebanon that grew once in Golgotha dust;
And Mary put down the phone at reception
With Gabriel's voice barking from the receiver.

Acknowledgements

Poems from this volume previously appeared in *Another Lost Shark/Stylus Poetry* (Australia) as well as two limited edition chapbooks by Alfred Gustav Press (*Reservations*, 2009) and Cactus Press (*Customs*, 2009).

I wish to acknowledge the Canada Council for the Arts, the British Columbia Arts Council, and the University of Oregon for their assistance.

About the Author

MATT RADER is the author to two previous collections of poetry, *Miraculous Hours* (2005), and *Living Things* (2008). His poems and stories have been published across North America, Europe, and Australia. He lives in the Comox Valley on Vancouver Island.

For A. F. R.

I am light and ready to travel.
I slept all day in the pews of the earth.
My name means Clearer of the Woods.